GRACE

Mick Gordon and A C Grayling

GRACE

OBERON BOOKS
LONDON

First published in 2006 by Oberon Books Ltd as *On Religion*
521 Caledonian Road, London N7 9RH
Tel: 020 7607 3637 / Fax: 020 7607 3629
e-mail: info@oberonbooks.com
www.oberonbooks.com

2nd edition as *Grace* 2008

ISBN: 978-1-84002-797-6

Characters

GRACE
A Professor of Natural Science. In her sixties.

TOM
Grace's son. Early thirties.

TONY
Grace's husband. Retired teacher.

RUTH
Tom's girlfriend. Early thirties.

The voice of DR MICHAEL PERSINGER
can be played by the actor playing Tony

The play should be performed straight through,
without an interval.

Scene 1

GRACE is sitting in Dr Michael Persinger's Transcranial Magnetic Stimulator. She sits with goggles over her eyes and wearing a yellow motorcycle helmet that has been fitted with electrodes. She looks like a surreally enthroned Pope.

Some time passes.

GRACE: Hello?

> *Several beats.*
>
> Hello?
>
> *Beat.*
>
> Is there someone…
>
> *Listening intently.*
>
> Is someone there?
>
> *A crackle of a loud speaker.*
>
> Tom?
>
> *The disembodied voice of the American scientist MICHAEL PERSINGER through the speaker.*

MICHAEL: Sorry Professor.

GRACE: Michael?

MICHAEL: Yes. I'm here Professor.

GRACE: Michael? I thought…

> *GRACE needs to lift her goggles to compose herself.*

GRACE: Sorry.

MICHAEL: Is everything alright?

GRACE: I'm just not sure this is working Michael. Nothing seems to be happening.

MICHAEL: No, Professor, you're right, nothing is happening.

GRACE: (*Expertly collecting herself.*) I can em, I can feel a sort of buzzing, slightly. Although that could be my ears – they buzz sometimes when I'm nervous.

MICHAEL: We're just completing the final checks. Thank you Professor, you're being extremely patient.

GRACE: Well if I'd known that having a religious experience was going to be as complicated as this I might actually have considered going to church! Buzzing's stopped.

MICHAEL: Good. Shall I talk you through the process?

GRACE: Do. Please.

MICHAEL: As you know all perception and thought is based on electrical activity in the brain.

GRACE: Yes. Right.

MICHAEL: What we're attempting to do is identify the specific electric pulses that cause specific brain reactions: one induces the mystical feelings we're trying for today, another a general feeling of well-being, another creates sexual arousal.

GRACE: Sexual arousal. I should have brought Tony.

MICHAEL: Who's Tony?

GRACE: My husband. Sorry. He has a sort of joke reflex. He'd find all this very amusing.

MICHAEL: The helmet itself isn't dangerous. But if you find yourself becoming frightened, then please, speak up.

GRACE: Of course.

MICHAEL: And we'll pause the experiment.

GRACE: Right.

MICHAEL: Even if you just start to feel slightly uncomfortable, please let us know.

GRACE: (*Too firmly.*) I've already said that I will Michael. Thank you.

MICHAEL: Sorry, I didn't mean to…

GRACE: No. No, of course you didn't. You didn't. I'm just… it's just… Thank you. You're being very kind Michael.

MICHAEL: You're most welcome Professor.

GRACE: Grace.

MICHAEL: Okay. Grace. Thank you. Well I think we're ready to go.

GRACE: (*Almost smiles.*) Through the looking glass.

GRACE puts the goggles on.

MICHAEL: If you like. Are you ready, Grace?

GRACE: As I'll ever be.

MICHAEL: Then we'll see you on the other side.

Sounds. Moves fluidly into:

Scene 2

GRACE's helmet experience. GRACE imagines a domestic scene in her Oxfordshire home. Perhaps she is sitting in her kitchen.

TONY: The Sky Spirit?

RUTH: Native Americans presumably.

GRACE: Right.

TONY: Right. Gosh.

GRACE: Different subjects tend to label the ghostly perception with the names that their cultures have taught them: Elijah, Jesus, the Virgin Mary, Mohammed, the Sky Spirit.

TOM: And who did you, y'know, did you see anyone?

GRACE: You don't *see* exactly.

TOM: No?

GRACE: No. They put big black goggles over your eyes and get you to stare at a red light.

TONY: Big black goggles?

GRACE: They're to reduce extraneous stimulation. Help the subject to concentrate. Apparently.

TONY: To concentrate?

GRACE: Yes. Then he talks you through the process...

TONY: So how can you see the light?

GRACE: What?

TONY: You said they get you to stare at a red light.

GRACE: Yes.

TONY: But if they put big black goggles over your eyes how can you see it?

Beat as GRACE thinks. Irritatingly, TONY has made a very good point.

GRACE: I... I don't know Tony, you just can. It must glow through the plastic or something.

TONY: I'm only asking.

TOM: How do they give it to you? The religious experience?

GRACE: You have to wear a sort of motorcycle helmet...

TONY: Motorcycle helmet?

GRACE: Which holds the electrodes in the correct position.

TONY: Electrodes?

GRACE: They call it the God Helmet.

TONY: The God Helmet?

GRACE: Yes. And will you please stop repeating everything I say. It makes it all sound ridiculous!

TONY: Does it? Sorry.

GRACE: Anyway, you were the one who told me to go.

TONY: Right.

GRACE: You don't *see* anything, it's more like feeling something, a presence.

TOM: Like a ghost?

GRACE: Some people do describe it like feeling the presence of a ghost. Basically what they do is stimulate the right hemisphere of the brain in the region that controls ideas of self, followed by the left hemisphere, the language centre, which interprets the stimulation as a sort of sensed entity.

TONY: And this man actually gets paid to do this?

GRACE: It's important work...

TONY: Right.

GRACE: Michael Persinger thinks it's this stimulation that's responsible for almost anything we sense as paranormal.

TOM: '*I see dead people!*'

RUTH: What's that from?

TOM: The one with thingy in it.

TONY: Well I for one prefer life to have a little more mystery. And I refuse to let anyone reduce my sense of the spiritual to brain static. Especially a Canadian.

GRACE: He's not a Canadian, he's an American

TONY: Well what's he doing in Canada then?

GRACE: It's just where he works.

TONY: Come off it. No one just works in Canada. It all sounds highly suspicious if you ask me.

GRACE: Well no one did dear.

TONY: The God Helmet.

TOM: So who did you see?

TONY: Talk about leading the witness.

GRACE: Sorry?

TOM: Who did you see?

RUTH: Sense.

TOM: Sense.

RUTH: *The Sixth Sense*! Bruce Willis!

TOM: Bruce Willis! So who did you sense Mum? Who did you sense?

Beat.

GRACE: (*To her son.*) You.

A moment between GRACE and TOM. TOM exits.

TONY: So who did you sense Grace?

GRACE: No. I... No. It didn't really work on me. I just sort of felt floaty and remembered the time you went down on me in the rowing boat.

RUTH: (*A little shriek of joy.*) Ah!

GRACE: What?

RUTH: Grace?

12

GRACE: Yes.

RUTH: In a rowing boat?!

GRACE: Yes!

TONY: Grace!

RUTH: And *Tony*?

TONY: What?

RUTH: In a rowing boat!

TONY: No.

GRACE: Oh stop being so coy. Yes, in a rowing boat!

RUTH: That is…!

TONY: Coy? I'm not being coy.

GRACE: It's fine when you're the one doing the talking.

RUTH: (*Delighted.*) Okay stop. This is getting disgusting.

GRACE: No it wasn't actually. I seem to remember it was totally fabulous.

TONY: I am not being *coy*. It's just that I've never been with you in a rowing boat.

GRACE: You bloody well have!

TONY: Honestly Grace, I haven't.

GRACE: You liar!

TONY: Never!

    Beat. Then GRACE suddenly remembers.

GRACE: Oh my God.

    Moves fluidly into:

Scene 3

Before. TOM has been rehearsing his summing up speech in front of RUTH.

RUTH: Come on. Again. And put some *passion* into it!

TOM: I hate this.

RUTH: Pretend you're thingy.

TOM: Thingy?

RUTH: The one in you know.

TOM: What?

RUTH: That film.

TOM: What film?

RUTH: You know the one I mean.

TOM: The guy's guilty as hell.

RUTH: Minorities need defending.

TOM: But why do I have to do it?

RUTH: Because you chose to!

TOM: Did I?

RUTH: If we're not standing by the vulnerable then why are we lawyers?

TOM: To get to the truth?

RUTH: Truth's an ironic concept in a criminal trial.

TOM: How can you say that?

RUTH: Because it's about *proof* not truth! (*Pointing.*) Tom Cruise.

TOM: I think you mean Jack Nicholson.

RUTH: No. Jack Nicholson's the other one.

TOM: Is he?

RUTH: (*Impression.*) 'You can't handle the truth!'

TOM: Woo. That is strangely erotic.

RUTH: But today not I...

TOM: But today not I, not the Prosecution Counsel, not the Judge...

RUTH: *Even...*

TOM: Not *even* the Judge can tell you what to do. Today ladies and gentlemen of the jury you are sovereign. And you must not convict my client unless you are sure beyond *all reasonable doubt* of his guilt. Now what does that mean – Reasonable Doubt? What does it mean? Absolutely nothing!

RUTH: Tom!

TOM: Did you know that modern Arabic has no word for Israeli so when they refer to Israelis they have to say Jews?

RUTH: He's going down for 50 years Tom. He's just a boy.

Beat.

TOM: Would you be able to say beyond reasonable doubt what you ate for lunch two weeks ago, the Tuesday before last say? I couldn't. Honestly I couldn't. Can you even say beyond reasonable doubt that your birthday is your birthday? I can't. In this country you have up to six weeks to register a birth. So up to six weeks after the most traumatic and jubilant event in an adult life your birth is registered by one of your parents. Now just look at my parents – how *reasonable* are they?

RUTH: You can't use the phrase directly.

TOM: What?

RUTH: Reasonable doubt, you mustn't say it, you'll sound like Perry Mason. (*Improvised and brilliant.*) Members of the jury, you have taken an oath to try this case on the *evidence*. And the prosecution must prove their case on the *evidence* presented to you in this court. Not on conjecture or surmise. Not on some vague notion of guilt by association. Not on difference. Not on commonsense expressions like 'there's no smoke without fire'. And not on the fear, the fear that we, all of us, sometimes feel in these extraordinary times. And the prosecution must prove their case to an incredibly high standard. They must make you, members of the jury, *sure*. What does that mean? How are we to know what *sure* means? Well it means that if you think the defendant *may* – be – guilty then it's your duty to acquit him. Your duty. Sworn on an oath.

Beat.

TOM: I don't think I can Ruth.

Beat.

RUTH: And it's Isra'eleen.

TOM: What is?

RUTH: Modern Arabic for Israeli.

TOM: Put your wig on.

RUTH: You have a one-track mind.

TOM: Thank you.

Moves fluidly into:

Scene 4

GRACE remembers giving a lecture. Perhaps we can hear sounds of a lecture theatre. Perhaps slides of William Paley then Charles Darwin...

GRACE: Imagine you're crossing a park, when you strike your foot against a small object. Instinctively you reach down to see what it is and you find yourself picking up a stone. As you look at it, you begin to wonder how the stone came to be there. And you come to the conclusion, that, for all you know, the stone has been there for ever.

Now suppose that when you reach down you don't find a stone beside your shoe, you find a *watch.* You pick it up, look at it and begin to wonder how it came to be there. Now you're hardly going to come to the same conclusion that you came to before: that for all you know, the watch has been there forever. No, not at all. The watch can't have been there forever because the watch must have had a maker. There must have existed, at some time or other, a *designer* of this watch.

And according to *William Paley* every manifestation of design that exists in the watch, exists in the stone. There's no difference, he says, except that in works of nature the degree of design is so sophisticated as to exceed all computation. And his conclusion is simple: The marks of design in nature are too strong to be ignored. And design must have a designer. And that designer, he insists, is God.

This classic historical argument for intelligent design is known as the Watchmaker Argument. And William Paley made it with passionate sincerity and he was informed by the best biological scholarship of the eighteenth century. But it is bollocks! Complete and utter BOLLOCKS!

The only watchmaker in nature is the *blind force of physics.* A true watchmaker has foresight: he designs his cogs and springs, and plans their interconnections with a future purpose in mind. *Natural Selection,* the blind unconscious, automatic process which Charles Darwin discovered has no purpose in mind. In fact it is purpose-*less*. It does not plan for the future. It has no vision, no foresight, no sight at all.

So if natural selection can be said to play the role of watchmaker in nature, it is the *Blind* Watchmaker.

A bell goes. Perhaps sounds of students packing up.

If anyone uses the term bollocks in their essay they will automatically fail.

Moves fluidly into:

Scene 5

GRACE remembers the summer's day that TOM first told her that he was going to become a priest. An Oxfordshire garden. TONY enters wearing a very old and definitely home-made Queen of Hearts costume including a crown. He is reading from an old script of Alice through the Looking Glass. *RUTH sits, enjoying TONY's performance.*

TONY: (*To GRACE as The Queen.*) 'Oh don't go on like that! Consider what a great girl you are. Consider what a long way you've come today. Consider anything, only don't cry!'

TOM enters wearing an old Alice costume from Alice through the Looking Glass, *including an Alice hair band. GRACE sits down to watch with RUTH, she is smiling.*

TOM: (*To TONY as Alice.*) '*Can* you keep from crying by considering things?'

TONY: 'That's the way it's done. Nobody can do two things at once you know. Let's consider your age to begin with – how old are you?'

TOM: 'Seven.'

GRACE: 'Seven and a half *exactly*.' Every time.

TONY: 'You needn't say exactly! I can believe it without that. Now I'll give *you* something to believe. I'm just one hundred and one, five months and a day.'

TOM: 'I can't believe *that*!'

TONY: 'Can't you? Try again, draw a long breath, and shut your eyes.'

TOM: (*TOM does so. It doesn't seem to work.*) 'There's no use trying. One *can't* believe impossible things.'

TONY: 'I dare say you haven't had much practice. When I was your age, I always did it for half an hour a day. Why, sometimes I've believed as many as...'

TONY/ GRACE / TOM: 'Six impossible things BEFORE BREAKFAST!!'

GRACE: Where did you find them?

TOM: My old room.

TONY: I'd have made a great Queen.

GRACE: Off with his head! Give me that. (*GRACE reclaims her crown.*)

TOM: (*To RUTH.*) What do you think? (*Does a twirl.*)

RUTH: You weren't.

TONY: He was you know.

TOM: (*Smiling at RUTH.*) I've always been extremely confident in my sexuality.

RUTH: You were Alice?

TOM falls dreamlike to the ground.

TONY: It's a family thing. Best not to ask too many questions.

TOM: We did it every summer. Grandpa organised it.

GRACE: My father. The Mad Hatter!

TONY: 'No room! No room!' I'd have made a great Mad Hatter.

GRACE: Oh sweetheart, always the bridesmaid...

TONY: Story of my life.

TOM: Don't believe a word of it. Dad stole the show.

TONY places his hand on his heart.

TONY: *Moi?*

RUTH: Who did you play?

GRACE: One guess.

RUTH: Now that's unfair!

TONY: No go on. Rrrrrrr... Purrrrrrrrrr...

TONY grins and in a very cat-like way gets down on his hands and knees and begins purring and crawling towards RUTH.

RUTH: Of course!

GRACE: Of course. Get up Tony and behave yourself. (*TONY gets up.*) It's very lovely to see you both.

TONY: It really is.

RUTH: Yes. Yes it is, isn't it Tom?

TOM: Yes, yes it's lovely.

RUTH looks expectantly at TOM.

GRACE: (*Smiling.*) What... What's going on?

TOM: Nothing.

RUTH: (*Forced smile.*) Well not nothing...

TONY: Are you two getting... (*married*)?

RUTH: No!

TOM: No! Honestly it's nothing. Just what happens when Ruth sees me in a dress. Her family never did anything like plays and things.

GRACE: Well that's hardly surprising love.

RUTH: Excuse me?

GRACE: You had more important things to deal with. From what I gather...

TONY: (*Clapping his hands together and rubbing them.*) So, drinks!

RUTH: Oh?

GRACE: From Tom. He told us about your mother...

RUTH: Oh.

TONY: I was thinking Pimms?

GRACE: How you were the one who found her.

TOM: Mum!

RUTH: Right.

GRACE: I'm sorry, I thought...

RUTH: No no. No, it's fine.

TONY: So Pimms all round then.

GRACE: I mean it's best to be upfront about these things don't you think?

RUTH: Em... Yes... Yes I do.

TOM: Welcome to *our* house...

RUTH: Well maybe I did have a lot to deal with. I don't know if I can say it was more than anyone else particularly...

GRACE: Well I'd have to disagree, love...

TOM: Where we're always *upfront* about things.

RUTH: (*To TOM.*) Oh really Tom?

Beat.

TONY: Back in a tick.

TONY exits.

GRACE: What was your mother's name?

RUTH: Chan.

GRACE: Chan?

RUTH: Kachanda. Little Sunflower.

GRACE: Little sunflower. That's beautiful.

TOM: Beautiful.

RUTH: *Tom!*

TOM: What?

RUTH looks at TOM, she is angry.

GRACE: My mother was called Sarah. Sadie. Loved her statues. Virgins everywhere. In many ways she was worse than Dad.

TOM: He did his best.

GRACE: Dad adored Tommy. Spoilt him rotten.

RUTH: Evidently.

TOM: I didn't leave the law because I was *spoilt...*

GRACE: Mmm. I was a horrible child *too.* Operated a split personality. Two wardrobes, two faces, two characters: one for home, one for the world. Home – boring: school projects, school uniform, school everything, more or less what you see today, but back then when I stepped out into the world it was mini-skirts, make-up, stilettos. Glamour all the way! It all had to be hidden in the shed of course. I used to change in the church.

RUTH: Stilettos in the church. How very radical.

GRACE: Not the building, it was always locked. The graveyard.

TOM: You haven't told me this.

GRACE: And I certainly didn't tell your grandfather.

RUTH: Tom said he hit you.

TOM: Ruth!

RUTH: (*To TOM.*) I'm just trying to be upfront.

GRACE: Yes. Yes of course you are. Yes of course she is. (*Now real respect.*) Very good. Yes. He did hit me. Sometimes. But the real punishment was left to *the good Lord*, and my guilt. Of which there was always plenty.

TOM: She makes him sound like some perverted old Bible basher. He wasn't.

GRACE: You didn't know him. Anyway, all he ever did was buy you sweeties.

RUTH: Changing in the graveyard. That would have been too scary for me.

GRACE: It was beautiful somehow. Beautifully kept. Lots of flowers. They employed a gardener. Nice man. Extremely *smelly*. Mr Kennedy. He used to piss on the geraniums. We liked to spy on him, see his willy. Occasionally Mr Kennedy would catch us watching and give chase. We got up to all sorts of mischief in there.

TOM: And Grandpa never knew?

GRACE: He never said anything. But he must have. One time I came home, I wasn't very old, fourteen maybe, and we'd been drinking cider and smoking cigarettes...

TOM: Cider and cigarettes!

GRACE: ...in skirts up to our ears. And this particular night, when I was supposed to be at some... I don't know, something biblical, I was pissed up in the graveyard getting it on with Kevin Johnston. He was the local stud. We called him *the initiator*.

TOM: Wow! Please! Too much information.

GRACE: So I was with *the initiator*, and I must have been terribly drunk because I forgot to change back into my other clothes. And I came home wearing, you know, well, not very much at all really, and I tried to have a conversation with him and he slapped me too hard that night because in the morning my face was swollen, so swollen *Tom*, I couldn't go to school. God the shame! Engulfed the house. He never said a word about it. Neither did I. Did you ever do that?

TOM: What?

GRACE: Sneak out and go drinking?

TOM: I just did it at home.

GRACE: I never noticed.

TOM: (*Flippantly.*) You were never there.

GRACE: (*Annoyed.*) I was there when you came back from America.

TOM: Don't remember that.

GRACE: Well I do!

TOM: I remember when I put the ecstasy into Dad's curry. Now that was a classic! I once spiked Dad's Chicken Korma with a crushed up E.

RUTH: What?

TOM: Yeah! Mum went absolutely mental and Dad was trying to bollock me but he couldn't stop smiling and giggling because he was getting all loved up!

GRACE: That was a bloody dangerous thing to do. Tony didn't know if he was coming or going.

TOM: (*Laughing.*) It was hilarious though!

GRACE really enjoys this memory and laughing with her son.

Dad loved it. He was trying to score off me for weeks after that.

GRACE: Your father...

TOM: Poor Dad.

GRACE: Do you think that's what it was?

TOM: What?

GRACE: That sent you to the Lord. All those drugs.

TOM: Let's not open that door.

GRACE: Fine.

TOM: It's a serious thing Mum.

RUTH: Yes. Yes it is. Isn't it Tom?

GRACE: Well I touched Bowie's sleeve once outside the London Palladium. Now that's a serious thing. And I'm pleased to tell you I am *still* extremely cool. The junior common room has just voted me the hippest scientist in college.

TOM: Only because you're a famous atheist.

GRACE: Don't.

TOM: Students always vote for atheists.

GRACE: I am not an atheist!

TOM: Okay, okay...whatever.

GRACE: Atheist, young man, is a religious term. Like pro-life. Like intelligent design. The word itself gives credence to the idea it is pretending to criticise. It's pernicious. Atheist is not a description, it's advertising. I am a naturalist.

RUTH is still looking at TOM. GRACE becomes aware.

No really you two. What the hell's going on?

TOM looks to RUTH.

RUTH: Upfront.

TOM smiles: this is why he loves RUTH.

TOM: I've got something to tell you Mum.

Beat.

Moves fluidly into:

Scene 6

The first anniversary of TOM's death. At the cemetery RUTH has brought a little bunch of flowers and TONY has brought a book and a stone to place. TONY takes a handkerchief out of his pocket and covers his head to say the Kaddish. RUTH stands a respectful distance from him and watches him. TONY cannot remember learning the Kaddish by ear and his reading sometimes falters but he will get through it.

TONY: Yeetgadal v' yeetkadash sh'mey rabbah.
   B'almah dee v'rah kheer'utey
   V'yamleekh malkhutei, b'chahyeykhohn, uv' yohmeyghohn,
   Uv'chahyei d'chohl beyt yisrael,
   Ba'agalah u'veez'man kareev, v'eemru: Amein.
   Y'hey sh'met rabbah m'varach l'alam u'l'almey almahyah.
   Yeet'barakh, v'yeesh'tabach, v' yeetrohmam, v' yeet'nasei,
   V' yeet'hadar, v' yeet'aleh, v' yeet'halal sh'mey d'kudshah b'reekh hoo.
   L'eylah meen kohl beerkhatah v'sheeratah,
   Toosh'b'...

Moves fluidly into:

Scene 7

GRACE remembers. The same day as Scene 5. Moments later.

GRACE: (*To TONY.*) Are you going to say anything to your son?

TONY: No.

GRACE: Tony!

TONY: It won't matter love. When has anyone ever done anything because of something someone else has said? I'm with Freud on this one. The only thing that motivates people is sex and aggression.

GRACE: You don't know the first thing about Freud.

TONY: I most certainly do.

GRACE: You do not.

TONY: I do.

TOM: You don't Dad.

TONY: Yes I do.

TOM: Name one thing you've read.

TONY: Don't be so silly, no one actually reads Freud.

RUTH: I read Freud.

TONY: Well that really is fucked up.

GRACE: You are *not* becoming a Priest!

TOM: I'm not asking your permission *Mother*, I'm telling you what I'm doing and asking what you think.

GRACE: An Anglican Priest! You're asking for a clip round the ear.

TONY: Just like I said, sex and aggression. All you need to understand.

TONY makes to leave.

GRACE: Shut up! And stay here!

TOM: I should have known better.

RUTH: You're doing fine.

GRACE: And what do you think about this?

RUTH: I don't know yet.

GRACE: You don't know yet? What about everything you stand for? What about the burden of proof? What about decisions based on *evidence*?

TOM: What do you mean you don't know yet?

RUTH: I don't know yet.

GRACE: (*From RUTH to TOM.*) Well I do and I'll tell you *exactly* what I think.

RUTH: Grace don't.

GRACE: Don't 'don't' me you coward!

TONY: Love!

GRACE: If my son wants to know what I think I'm going to tell him exactly what I think because thought is the precise ingredient most lacking in this ridiculous situation. What I think is, *Tom*, what I think is that your ignominious toying with faith has always been an extremely irritating adolescent reaction to this family and not just to me but also your father but that this, this latest idea of yours, this *decision* of yours, and at your age…you're too old for this type of teenage revenge. It's ridiculous Tom. It's absurd!

TOM: I know you'll find this hard to believe Mum, but my decision is not actually about you.

TONY: (*To RUTH.*) She will find that hard to believe.

TOM: And what about you?

28

TONY: What about me?

TOM: What do you think?

TONY: What do I think?

TOM: *Dad!*

Beat as TONY thinks.

TONY: I don't give a shit.

GRACE: Oh for Christ's sake *Tony!*

TONY: Well I don't.

TOM: What do you mean you don't give a shit?

TONY: I mean I don't give a shit.

TOM: You had me circumcised.

TONY: That's completely different. That was cultural. To save you from embarrassment in the bathroom.

TOM: Embarrassment in the bathroom?

TONY: You would have thought you were weird. You'd have looked at me then looked at yourself and thought you were weird. Deformed. Had a growth. All sons compare themselves to their fathers. They can't help it.

RUTH: I've never been a fan of foreskins, they're pointless and they're ugly.

TONY: (*Pointing finger at RUTH as if to tick her off.*) I am starting to like you more and more.

RUTH: Thank you.

TONY: Welcome to the family!

GRACE: You're completely deluded. Why did I marry you?

TONY: Because you love me. Now is anyone else peckish?

GRACE: Completely and utterly deluded.

TOM: Sons do not always compare themselves to their fathers.

TONY: Yes they do. It's in the brain. Evolution. Ask your mother about it.

GRACE: Actually he's right.

TONY: (*Grinning.*) See!

GRACE: I don't know what you think you have to grin about.

TOM: (*To GRACE.*) How could you have let that happen?

GRACE: I didn't let it happen. (*To TONY.*) Your father did it all by himself while I was at work. And do you know what he said to me when I came home?

TONY: (*Delighted, to RUTH.*) I've got a surprise for you!

RUTH: Tony!

GRACE: I've got a surprise for you!

RUTH: You are a truly terrible man.

TONY: Thank you.

GRACE: I have *mutilated* your child.

TONY: I have saved your child from years of psychological trauma not to mention several potential hygiene issues.

GRACE: He gets it from you.

TONY: How does he get it from me? He doesn't want to be a Rabbi does he?! Why don't you want to be a Rabbi? I can't believe I just asked that. But seriously, why don't you want to be... (*RUTH closes her eyes and looks down. TONY firmly interrupts himself.*) No! Stop it! Please everyone, ignore me.

TOM: I'm doing the training whatever *any* of you think. This isn't me just fiddling in my bath. I'm serious. Very serious. There's 2000 years of scholarship and questioning, 2000 years of inspiration and exploration...

GRACE: What's wrong son?

TOM: Nothing's *wrong.*

GRACE: This is all my fault. That summer when you went off to America to build those houses. That was the beginnings of this.

TOM: No! (*Don't start this again…*)

GRACE: That cunt creationist born again fuckwit!

TONY puts his head in his hands.

TOM: He was a *lunatic!*

GRACE: (*Correcting him.*) He was a *lunatic!* He gave you all those pamphlets and you were completely seduced. He targeted you Tom. He knew you were my son.

TOM: I thought you'd at least be happy for me.

GRACE: How could you possibly think I'd be happy for you?

TOM: I don't know.

GRACE: We've given you *everything.* You have wanted for *nothing.* What is wrong? Something must be *wrong.*

TOM: *Nothing is wrong!*

RUTH: I'm pregnant.

Sudden silence. This is clearly news to them all. TOM and GRACE are both stunned. TONY is the first to recover, somewhat in awe of RUTH.

TONY: Well… Right… Well that really is… No, that's… Congratulations… (*Laughs.*) *Mazeltov!* (*Catches himself.*) Well, congratulations…

RUTH: Thank you Tony…

TONY: No really… I mean it… *Congratulations…*Honestly, to both of you. *Really.*

RUTH: Tom.

TOM: Sorry?

RUTH: Tony's...

TONY: From both of us, really...

TOM: Yeah?

RUTH: (*Nodding and grinning back.*) Yeah.

> *GRACE forgets herself and grabs RUTH to her.*

TONY: Congratulations son! *Congratulations!!*

> *A beautiful moment then the crackle of Michael Persinger's loudspeaker. Lights close to GRACE, who looks up.*

MICHAEL: Shall we continue Professor? Shall we go on?

> *Beat.*

> Grace. Do you want to go on?

GRACE: Yes. Yes, we should...

MICHAEL: Okay. Three, two...

> *Moves fluidly into:*

Scene 8

GRACE remembers rehearsing a lecture. TONY is doing Sudoku.

GRACE: One: Explanations. Answers to the basic questions about the origins of the universe. Two. Comfort. Reassurance in a hostile world. Three. Cohesion. They consolidate communities and bring a useful sense of order. And four. Superstition.

TONY: There are too many numbers in it. Numbers make people nervous.

GRACE: But there is of course a *fifth* reason offered. A reason which says that religions exist because there is a god, or gods, and belief is simply a response to that fact. This tends to be religion's own answer. What *do* you think about it?

TONY: It's good. And you're right, the numbers do help.

GRACE: No. About Tom.

TONY: Oh…yes, well you know, I was surprised but I have to say I'm genuinely very happy for him. I am! I mean I think it was a bit of a shock, but he'll be a great dad and she's *smashing…*

GRACE: No Tony. This Priest *crap*?

TONY: Oh, right, yes, right, that. Well I mean, look on the bright side. Who's going to take a priest called Friedman seriously?

GRACE: *Tony?*

TONY: He's got a degree in philosophy. What did you expect?

GRACE: A rationalist!

TONY: Ha!

GRACE: I just can't understand.

TONY: 'Know then thyself; presume not God to scan;
The proper study of mankind is man.'

GRACE: Damn right. Who is that?

TONY: The Pope.

GRACE: The Pope? Which Pope?

TONY: There is only one Pope – Alexander Pope.

GRACE: Answer my question.

TONY: Em, well, you know, Tom's always been a romantic.

GRACE: So have you.

TONY: But he's cleverer than me and he's had way too much education so I can see why he likes Christianity over

Judaism, I mean…the holy trinity and all that…takes some mental gymnastics that god in three parts stuff – I guess it's sufficiently complicated for him and I don't know, he seems happy, can't you hate the sin and love the sinner?

GRACE: I feel like a failure.

TONY: Oh love, don't.

GRACE: Don't tell me what to feel Tony.

TONY: Then don't tell Tom what to believe! If anyone tried telling you what to think you'd hate it. And it doesn't matter that you're right, it doesn't matter at all, it's not the point, he's finding his own way, exploring and questioning and he's trying to involve us, which is a damn sight more that either of us did with our parents, so give him a bit of respect for that at least. He's going to do what he wants with or without us, so come on: 'Sweet moderation, heart of this nation…'

Enter TOM.

TOM: 'Desert us not we are between the wars.' Billy Bragg.

TONY: Great man.

GRACE: But are you disagreeing with me?

TONY: No I'm not, I'm just adding a bit of popular culture to the proceedings.

GRACE: Because I don't think you understand how important this is to me.

TONY: I really do.

TOM: What's this?

GRACE: In our world. With what we are capable of…

TONY: One guess.

GRACE: The violence we are capable of…

TONY: Did you know that the Dalai Lama fixes watches?

GRACE: What?

TONY: I thought you could use it in the Blind Watchmaker bit. He's mad on small gadgets apparently. Loves repairing them.

TOM: Really?

TONY: Apparently.

GRACE: Where do you get this stuff from?

TONY: No idea.

GRACE: So what are we going to do?

TONY: About what?

GRACE: (*Pointing at her son.*) Him!

TONY: Nothing. Be nice.

GRACE: Be nice?

TONY: Yes.

GRACE: Be *nice*?

TONY: Because he's our son

GRACE: I thought we watch the news together Tony. Don't we? How many die? How many? And for gods. For gods! It's the twenty-first century for Christ's sake!

TONY: Don't open that door.

GRACE: (*Exasperated by TONY's reply. To TOM. Very direct.*) You bear a heavy responsibility in all of this.

TOM: How?

GRACE: Because your lot provide cover for these nutters.

TONY: You'll regret this Grace.

GRACE: *Be nice!* (*Back to TOM.*) It's the heart of the issue. The basic problem. Because you and your religious moderation serve as a fig-leaf for religious extremism. Religious moderates – if there really can be such a thing which I very much doubt when push comes to *divine* shove – religious moderates, bear a huge responsibility for encouraging religious violence, because their language and beliefs...

TOM: My language and beliefs.

TONY leaves them to it.

GRACE: Yes son. Yes! Because your... (*After TONY.*) Coward! Because your language and your beliefs provide the context in which scriptural literalism and religious violence can never be adequately opposed.

TOM: Yeah.

GRACE: What do you mean *yeah*?

TOM: I mean yeah. It's a problem. It haunts me. Do I provide cover for the nutters?

GRACE: Yes.

TOM: For the fanatics.

GRACE: Yes.

TOM: For the lunatics?

GRACE: Yes!

TOM: Yes! Am I defending a whole y'know, which actually has about it all sorts of things I loathe. I *hate* the violent...but I think, and I'm becoming quite convinced, that the dangerous situation to get into is to see the world as a battle between those that have religion and those that don't. Where those that have religion are defined as zealots. Whereas for me, there's a really important role for those who want to say, we need to have *better* religion.

GRACE: That's just selfish Tom.

TOM: No it's not. It's not *selfish.*

GRACE: It's the excuse that allows you to hold on to this absurd leap of faith you make!

TOM: No! What I'm trying to do is to help people feel that it's fine to be thinking, moderate, self-critical *and* religious. And they're not the most dangerous people in the world Mum, they're not the ones to lose sleep over. If I provide cover I provide cover for that lot. I don't provide cover for sexist, homophobic, bigoted people who put bombs on planes. I did that when I was a lawyer! But life is complicated, and even the most ardent atheist...

GRACE: I am *not* an atheist!

TOM: Okay, okay, you know what I mean! Even the most ardent *naturalist* has to admit that life's not straightforward. I am an enlightenment person and I'm religious.

GRACE: That's a contradiction in terms.

TOM: Exactly! And I live with that. That's what I am.

GRACE: No. You can't have it both ways. It's faith *or* reason – you have to *choose.*

TOM: It's not a matter of which side I'm on.

GRACE: Son. Grow up! Yes it is!

TOM: Contradictions are what people are, bundles of contradictions, fighting them and working them out. And I refuse to be dictated to by your overly simplistic logic-chopping approach to life.

GRACE: I beg your pardon?

TOM: *Well* – you always want to limit experience to the cold theoretical but I'm telling you – the truth has to be sieved in lots of different ways.

GRACE: No! No it doesn't! It's exactly this kind of *slippery* talk that needs attacking: Talk that allows religion to demand

being treated *reasonably*. Because it shouldn't be. Because
religion is *not reasonable*. Rigorous rationality, proportioning
belief to evidence, may be cold, simplistic, *logic-chopping*!
But it's the only outlook we can truly rely on.

TOM: So let's take religion out of society.

GRACE: You're not listening.

TOM: And while you're about it, let's take away sex. Dad's
right about that, sex and aggression, it's what most of the
fights are about on Saturday night. So let's get rid of it.
Let's do test-tubes.

GRACE: I am not advocating a fascist state where everyone
walks around in white suits and smiles.

TOM: I don't live in your world Mum. I live in the real world
where religion is present everywhere.

GRACE: And that's precisely the problem. Because the
ultimate basis of religious morality – whatever up-dated
gloss you put on it – is divine command. Well it's too
dangerous!

TOM: I'm not trying to pretend that it's not dangerous
sometimes. I think that's absolutely the case. But I'm trying
to be realistic and pragmatic here, okay, because we have
to ask ourselves: is the answer to bad religion – practically
– no religion or better religion? Who's more likely to
defeat bad religion? Good religion or atheism? Now that's
a question. A *real* question. So stop attacking me because
I'm your hope! Because you're never going to turn the
world's religious into atheists. If that's what your battle is. If
that's what you are trying to do, you're going to lose. The
best we can hope for is to turn bad violent religion into
better religion and that's what I'm trying to do. So no, I'm
not providing cover for the nutters! And by wasting your
time attacking me it's your absurd *purism* which is letting
them off the hook because you're never going to win that
battle.

GRACE: We've made too many concessions to religious belief. It's the most pernicious source of conflict in our world today and you, my son, are one of its salesman.

TOM: And you're the fundamentalist.

GRACE: Fuck you!

Beat. TOM exits.

Tom. Tom come back. Tom!

TONY enters.

TONY: Only me.

GRACE: Sorry. I thought…

TONY: No.

GRACE: I couldn't stop myself Tony.

TONY: Neither could he by the sound of it.

GRACE: Why couldn't I stop myself?

TONY: Because it's important.

GRACE: (*As if correcting.*) Yes it is.

TONY bear-hugs GRACE.

TONY: Come here!

GRACE: Ohhhh…

TONY: It'll be alright.

GRACE: Will it?

TONY: We'll all go out for a curry. Take some ecstasy.

GRACE: D'you remember that?

TONY: Every time I hear music with a drum beat.

TONY does his dance move. GRACE laughs.

GRACE: I know what I should have said. When I was a student we had this professor, ancient man, Dr John R Baker. And for as long as anyone could remember he had taught that the Golgi Apparatus...

TONY: The what?

GRACE: The Golgi Apparatus. It's a feature of the interior of cells.

TONY: What does it do?

GRACE: It doesn't matter.

TONY: Right.

GRACE: It's not important love. The point is that Dr Baker taught that this thing wasn't real. For years he'd argued the same thing. Anyway, one day we had a lecutre from an American cell biologist. And to our growing shock and embarrassment we began to realise that he was presenting completely convincing evidence that the Golgi Apparatus was real. The whole room was avoiding making eye contact with Dr Baker. It was awful. And do you know what he did at the end of the lecture? At the end of the lecture the old man stood up and strode to the front of the hall, grabbed the American by the hand and with tears in his eyes said, 'My dear fellow, I wish to thank you, I have been wrong these 25 years.' We were all stunned. Stunned. And I felt very, very ashamed because of what I guess I'd thought my own reaction would've been if I'd been in his shoes. I clapped my hands red. I remember it like it was yesterday. Now that's a serious response to the world. A response on which we can place our moral compass. I should have told Tom that.

TONY: 'My dear fellow, I wish to thank you, I have been wrong these 25 years.' Nice. Classy.

GRACE: No religious person could ever say that.

Moves fluidly into:

Scene 9

Later. TOM and RUTH are sitting, alone.

TOM: Brian.

RUTH: Edward.

TOM: Derek.

RUTH: John.

TOM: Norman

RUTH: Robert.

TOM: That was Grandpa's name.

RUTH: Oh sorry!

TOM: Doesn't matter. *Kevin.*

RUTH: *Kevin.* Definitely. Anything pop star-ish.

TOM: Absolutely. Anything Politiciany.

RUTH: Richard, Ted or Dick.

TOM: Goes without saying. Pubert.

RUTH: Pubert?

TOM: Pubert.

RUTH: (*Okay then.*) Archibald.

TOM: Fester.

RUTH: Elvis.

TOM: Lurch.

RUTH: The Addams Family!

TOM: The Addams Family. If it's a girl.

RUTH: Maureen.

TOM: Sharon.

RUTH: Tandy.

TOM: Olive.

RUTH: Olive's not a name.

TOM: Yes it is. Someone I know has an aunt called Olive.

RUTH: Really?

TOM: Yup.

RUTH: OK. Olive or anything vegetably.

TOM: Or anything flowery. Lilly, Poppy, Bluebell...

RUTH: Rose.

TOM: Oh I like Rose.

RUTH: Nothing flowery you said.

TOM: An Olive isn't a vegetable you know.

RUTH: (*Lying.*) I know. And nothing herby.

TOM: Herby!

RUTH: No. Like Sage or something.

TOM: What about Chan?

Beat.

RUTH: Oh.

Beat.

I never thought of that. How weird.

TOM: Kachanda. Beautiful.

RUTH: It is flowery though.

TOM: Special dispensation. I really like it.

RUTH: I really like you.

TOM: Yeah?

RUTH: Yeah. Mostly.

They kiss.

Tom I'm finding all this priest…you know…

TOM: Yeah?

RUTH: Yeah, a bit.

TOM: Yeah… Guess where Dad took me?

RUTH: Bengal Tiger.

TOM: Yeah. And we started talking and I told him I was going to ask you to marry me.

Beat.

RUTH: What?

TOM: Yeah!

RUTH: Tom?

TOM: Yeah. And he said to me are you sure you're doing the right thing?

RUTH: *What?*

TOM: Yeah.

RUTH: It's a little late for that isn't it? (*Indicating pregnancy.*)

TOM: That's what I said.

RUTH: That's your bloody mother that is.

TOM: No it's not. He said it's what fathers are supposed to do.

RUTH: It's your mother.

TOM: So we'd had a few beers and I tell Dad what I'm planning and he says are you sure you're doing the right thing? And then he said pass me that napkin, so I passed him the napkin and he said, down the middle, draw a line down the middle and put all the sort of pluses and all the minuses for why this is a good thing. And so I drew all this and I tried to write down all the pluses...so y'know, she's cute and stuff...

RUTH: *She's cute!*

TOM: And stuff.

RUTH: Tom!

TOM: Lots of stuff!

RUTH: Have you still got this napkin?

TOM: Stop it. Listen to me. So you do the whole list of things and then you suddenly realise, or I did at least, I realised that that list could never add up to what I was about to do. However poetic or intelligent or clever or in touch with my own emotions I was, the sum total of that list on the plus side could never equal: I love this person – and want to marry them forever.

RUTH: Tom, you know how much I love you.

TOM: Yes. And it's why I need to explain this. That there comes a point when my justifications just run out, but I know that becoming a priest is just what I have to do. Just like I do about marrying you. I just *know*. And that's the area where my faith is located and it's not on the list.

RUTH: Is this a proposal Tom because if it is, I mean, do you really expect me to say yes?

TOM: I'm serious.

RUTH: So am I.

TOM: I know you're finding this difficult and you're being brilliant to me but I really want you to understand and the nearest analogy to it I think I can find is love. Love. You're going to give away your whole life, commit your whole life to this one person on the basis of this feeling. And what is it, this feeling? You could produce an expert to say, to reduce love, to some sort of chemical imbalance in the brain or to some sort of sociological need or whatever it is, you could do that so as to undermine, well I'd say, thank you, thank you very much but actually I'm still not interested, this love is more real to me than however true those explanations are, so there's something not on the list, something that exceeds the list, and I give myself over to that. Do you see? Is it better to be in love or not in love? I dunno. I'm in love. And it's not on the list.

RUTH: Because I don't believe in God Tom. And I really don't. And maybe I won't mind church – sometimes – because I like the rituals somehow. But I don't believe and I don't want you to try and persuade me, or our children. Is that going to be too difficult for you?

TOM: I'm not sure I *believe* in God, that God *exists*. I'm really not sure existence is the right word. The closer I get to it the less it seems to be there. But it just won't go away.

RUTH: Is that going to be too difficult for you?

TOM: It won't leave me alone Ruth. People think religion makes people *happy*! But it doesn't. It doesn't make me happy. I think the thing that makes most people happy in the world, and this is my theory...

TONY runs in to centre stage. GRACE sits.

TONY: No! This is my theory!

TOM: Dancing!

TONY: Dancing!

Loud music starts and TONY starts dancing as if on E. The music should continue under the dialogue until marked.

Dancing is what really makes people happy. It's got everything, it's got human contact, it's got other people, its got sex, it's got a bit of movement, it's got everything, physical, y'know, dancing is it, and yeah I think pretty much – dancing is what makes people happy. Oi – What's this? (*TONY moves his arms and legs as if he is a jellyfish.*) God moving in a mysterious way! Ha!

TOM is now dancing as well. Perhaps RUTH is starting to join in as the two scenes blend.

RUTH: The day after you first stayed over at mine. Do you remember?

TOM: Of course! I wooed you with my move. (*Does the move.*)

RUTH: The next day I called Laura and told her I thought you were a really good dancer!

TOM: Little did you know.

RUTH: One-move Friedman.

TOM: Thank you! (*He does his move.*)

RUTH: And when we spent that first Christmas with your parents I realized who you'd stolen it from.

TONY: One-move Friedman! (*TONY does the move.*)

GRACE: Tony sit down.

RUTH: I like your Dad.

TONY: You're not alone.

GRACE: *Tony.* You'll have a heart attack.

TONY: Right.

TONY sits down beside GRACE.

TOM: It's like in the... (*He can't remember the name of the film so does some crap kung fu moves as a prompt.*)

RUTH: *The Matrix.*

TOM: *The Matrix!* The first one, the others are rubbish, you fell asleep I think but the first *Matrix* is a great film.

RUTH: I didn't fall asleep. I took *you* to see that film.

TOM: Are you sure?

RUTH: Tom.

TOM: Really? It's very self-consciously religious, y'know…

RUTH: I know.

TOM: Trinity and so forth…

RUTH: God, you're unbelievable.

TOM: And Keanu Reeves gets born again and stuff, but…but there's a line in it where what's his name…

RUTH: Neo.

TOM: Yeah Neo, Neo's sitting there with – who's the black guy? – just before he takes this pill…

RUTH: Morpheus.

TOM: Morpheus…and he says something like um… I can remember *exactly* the line, he says 'You've had it, haven't you, a splinter in the mind', he says 'you have a splinter in the mind'. 'This splinter in the mind that you've never known quite what to do with, you've never quite known what it is, and its this thing that you just can't…' 'And the splinter in the mind is the…' something, this is not quite it, y'know, and you take the red pill and you get to see it, or you get the blue pill and you go back to how you were. So do you take the red pill or the blue pill? And that's what I've got, a splinter in the mind, that just won't go away. Do I sound crazy?

RUTH: Bonkers.

TOM: I love you. And I know you love me.

RUTH: I'm reconsidering.

TOM: Marry me.

RUTH: Is it going to be too difficult for you that I don't believe in God?

The music stops. Beat. The scenes move fluidly between RUTH's reality and GRACE's reality which is the day after TOM's death. Though from this point GRACE and TONY should never refer directly to TOM.

TONY: And what did he say?

TOM: Is it going to be too difficult for you that I do?

RUTH: (*To GRACE.*) He didn't reply.

TOM: Marry me.

GRACE: And what did you say?

TOM: Marry me Ruth.

RUTH: He didn't ask.

TONY: Oh.

TOM: *Ruth!*

TONY: Oh, I'm so sorry love.

TOM: Marry me.

RUTH: Yeah.

TONY: Shit.

RUTH: Yeah.

TONY: Shit. But do you know...what he would have wanted?

TOM: Hold on.

TOM gets a poetry book.

RUTH: Yeah.

GRACE: He means for the funeral.

RUTH: I know.

GRACE: You do?

RUTH: He wanted it at St Peter's.

GRACE: St Peter's.

RUTH: He thought it was beautiful. A serious place.

TONY: (*Understanding.*) Right.

GRACE: No.

TONY: (*Agreeing with GRACE.*) Right.

RUTH: That's what he wanted.

TOM: Here we go. Page 58. This is what I'm trying to say.

GRACE: No way.

TOM: It's beautiful.

GRACE: It's terrible. We can't.

TONY: No. Right.

GRACE: I mean we just can't. In a church!

RUTH: That's what he wanted.

TOM: 'Once I am sure there's nothing going on
I step inside, letting the door thud shut.
Another church…'

GRACE: No. No. A private ceremony is enough.

RUTH: Enough? Would Tom think it was enough?

GRACE: Ruth. The people who did this, the people who
murdered my…who murdered all those innocent, they…

RUTH: Tom wasn't killed because of what he believed Grace.

GRACE: Tom was killed…

RUTH: Because he was there! Just because he was…

GRACE: Ruth. Think! Be reasonable.

RUTH: How? *How?*

GRACE: It's wrong. We can't.

TOM: And he goes through what he does in this church and he looks around and em and...

'...Mounting the lectern, I peruse a few
Hectoring large-scale verses, and pronounce
"Here endeth" much more loudly than I'd meant.'

RUTH: My Mum was an atheist. I buried her. Organised her funeral. She was, I don't know, she hated religion. She hated most things really. And at the funeral we didn't say a word because it wasn't right. Because she would have hated it. So we said nothing. And it wasn't enough. It really wasn't. Not nearly. And I don't pretend to share what Tom believed but at the service... There's something I'd like you to read Tony. If you think you can. You probably know it. I'd do it but I don't think I'd manage... It's Larkin. And it's the end of...it's in here somewhere...

RUTH gets a second book, identical to the one TOM is reading from.

GRACE: Ruth the people who did this...

RUTH: I'm going to bury Tom the way he wanted.

GRACE: No.

RUTH: We have to.

GRACE: I won't have it!

TONY: Grace, love.

GRACE: (*Panic.*) Tony help me! Please!

RUTH: We have to.

TONY: Look we're all...

GRACE: NO!

RUTH: YES!

TONY: *STOP!* Both of you! Just absolutely stop!

TOM: 'Yet stop I did: in fact I often do,
   And always end much at a loss like this,
   Wondering what to look for; wondering, too,
   When churches fall completely out of use
   What we shall turn them into...'

RUTH: (*Searching the book. She is clearly in shock.*) It's called
   'Church Going', it's a poem called 'Church Going', it's
   about Larkin going into a church, page 58. Where he talks
   about what will happen in the...

TOM: In the future...

RUTH: In the future...

   RUTH starts to cry but controls herself by finding the place.

TOM: Where he says superstition, like belief, must die and I
   think that's probably wrong, and I think that Larkin does
   too because of what he says at the end...

RUTH: From here.

TONY: 'A serious house on serious earth it is...'

RUTH: That's it.

TOM: That's it.

   TOM exits.

TONY: 'A serious house on serious earth it is,
   In whose blent air all our compulsions meet,
   Are recognised, and robed as destinies.
   And that much never can be obsolete,
   Since someone will forever be surprising
   A hunger in himself to be more serious,
   And gravitating with it to this ground,
   Which, he once heard, was proper to grow wise in,
   If only that so many dead lie round.'

GRACE: We can't do this Ruth.

RUTH: We have to.

GRACE: No.

RUTH: If you deny Tom the funeral he wanted, I swear to Christ Grace, you will not be part of your grandchild's life.

The crackle of Michael Persinger's loudspeaker.

RUTH: Did you hear what I said?

MICHAEL: Can you hear me Professor?

GRACE: Sorry?

RUTH: Because I promise you Grace.

GRACE: (*Putting her hands to her ears.*) Yes. I heard you.

MICHAEL: We can hear *you* Professor. Is everything all right? Grace? Is everything all right?

Moves fluidly into:

Scene 10

After. GRACE remembers giving a public lecture.

GRACE: It is true that I don't speak passionately about the Norse Gods. This is because nobody believes in them anymore. But I probably would if I lived with people who believed in them and were killing each other in the name of Thor and Wotan. But belief in Jesus is rife in the world and belief in Allah is rife in the world. And people like my son have died because of it.

The United States is run now by born-again Christians, by people who act because they think that their prayers are being answered. In America, in a presidential election, an actor who reads the Bible would almost certainly defeat a rocket scientist who does not. And that country is our world's policeman. And what are they currently in charge of policing? Islamism. Islamism is not the moderate self-critical belief system that my son preached for. Islamism is a credal wave that calls for our own elimination. Every jihadi sees the need for eliminating all non-Muslims either by conversion or by execution. And the most extreme Islamists want to kill everyone on earth except the most extreme Islamists.

It is now time to reverse the prevailing notion that religious commitment is intrinsically deserving of respect. It is now time to refuse to tiptoe around those people who claim deference, consideration, special treatment, or any other kind of immunity on the grounds that they have a religious faith. As if having faith were a privilege-endowing virtue. As if it were noble to believe in unsupported claims and ancient superstitions. It is not a virtue. It is not noble. To believe something in the face of evidence and against reason – to believe something by faith – is ignoble, irresponsible and ignorant. And merits the opposite of respect.

Moves fluidly into:

Scene 11

Before. TONY has taken TOM for a curry.

TOM: It's like saying, speaking English…we don't have to affirm our Englishness by denying French or Urdu. What do I want to deny other languages for? I want to see religions as languages for talking about the divine. And if you see them as languages, Christianity doesn't contradict Islam just as English doesn't contradict French.

TONY: But Christianity does contradict Islam doesn't it? I mean Islam says Jesus was a minor prophet and Christianity says that he was the son of God. That sounds like a big difference to me.

TOM: I don't mean it like that. I'm not a literalist. I'm saying that the two religions are separate and equally valid approaches to dealing with the divine.

TONY: 'The sigh of the oppressed creature, the heart of a heartless world, the soul of soulless conditions.'

TOM: 'The opium of the people.'

TONY: Great man.

TOM: It's Mum's language I'm having trouble with.

TONY: Right.

TOM: It's why I'm always stuffed in conversations with her. Every point has a number. Everything must be clear. All problems answered by a league table. It's radical empiricism! I mean, do you really want to live in a world like that? I don't.

TONY: Oh dear...

TOM: Why do you love her so much?

TONY: Bloody good question.

TOM: I'm serious.

TONY: So am I.

TOM: Dad.

TONY: Fear.

TOM: Dad.

TONY: Really. A great aphrodisiac, fear.

TOM: Come on.

TONY: Admiration I think.

TOM: What?

TONY: Yeah. I've always admired your mother. It's true she has an unfortunate manner sometimes, but y'know, I've always thought she was right about stuff.

TOM: Really? Right?

TONY: Yeah. And her commitment. To what she believes, what she wants for the world. You know. Her hopes. You becoming a priest is genuinely very difficult for her.

TOM: I know. I've let her down.

TONY: No don't. Of course you haven't...

TOM: I couldn't stop myself.

TONY: Yeah. Well. It's important to you.

TOM: (*As a correction.*) *Yes it is.*

TONY: It'll be alright.

TOM: Will it?

TONY: We'll all go out for a curry. Take some ecstasy.

TOM: D'you remember that?

TONY: Every time I hear... You don't have any do you?

TOM: What?

TONY: E.

TOM: No!

TONY: I'm only asking.

TOM: Dad! I'm going to be a priest!

TONY: Yeah. A priest...called *Friedman!* Oy vey Maria!

Father and son have hysterics. Out of which...

TOM: Why did you never...you know?

TONY: Me?

TOM: Yeah.

TONY: Don't know really. It just never made much sense to me. And you know I'm just an old lefty at heart. I approve of the values, some of them, the compassion, but on the whole I see more evidence for its lack and I don't really approve of the structure and...you know, I'm too petty and schoolboy to resist the wind-up. The only religion I really enjoy is Hinduism and that's purely because it annoys religious Jews so much because it's just so much older than anything else. They hate that. And I love it that they hate it. Sad but true. Keeps me going. And there's other things too like the Hindu stories are more colourful and it's got no founder and there are lots of gods to choose from and it kind of admits it's a messy indefinable thing and of course I couldn't do it because apart from anything I'd miss the beef! But don't get me wrong, all that's positive and bollocks, I like it best because it pisses off the Orthodox. And Christianity is tricky – and I'm very proud of you and all that – and I don't think you're turning on the gas or anything, I mean I hope you know that, and I can see it makes you happy and that's more or less good enough for me, but Christianity you know... Tricky, and not just because of the historical example it has set in its relation to power – barbaric! And it's fine now and everything because the church has no teeth and that's exactly the way it should be if you ask me, but it's because of sin and punishment and is it really very humane to believe in everlasting punishment and I don't know but, and I'm sorry for being all Jewish all of a sudden but it's because at some point it, y'know all this son, Christianity does become personal to Jews because eventually it's the Jews who get the blame for bungling the initial you know, the thing.

TOM: The Crucifixion?

TONY: Yeah. Exactly. So there you go. That's me. Tony Friedman on religion. I'm starving where's our food?

TOM: I just really want Mum to understand that's all.

TONY: She might not son.

TOM: I know…

TONY: Just give her some time to get used to the idea.

TOM: Yeah.

TONY: Yeah. I like Ruth. I really do. She *scares* me a little. Smashing girl.

TOM: Dad!

TONY: Yeah. Smashing. How is she?

TOM: Loves being pregnant.

TONY: Your mother was the same. Bloody hell. Women. How do they survive their bodies?

TOM: I'm going to ask her to marry me.

TONY: Good.

TOM: You think?

TONY: Absolutely. Though if your mother was here she'd want me to make sure you're doing the right thing.

TOM: It's a bit late for that isn't it?

TONY: Yeah but no harm in thinking. Pass me that napkin.

Moves fluidly into:

Scene 12

TOM's funeral.

RUTH: I'm going to read something by Tom's favourite poet. Philip Larkin. It reminds me of Tom, because he used to recite it to me and…and it's for Tony and especially for

Grace who should take full responsibility for today's *private* ceremony.

'They fuck you up, your mum and dad,
They may not mean to, but they do.
They fill you with the faults they had,
And add some extra, just for you.

But they were fucked up in their turn
By fools in old-style hats and coats,
Who half the time were soppy-stern,
And half at one another's throats.

Man hands on misery to man.
It deepens like a coastal shelf.
Get out as early as you can,
And don't have any kids yourself.'

Moves fluidly into:

Scene 13

Some time after TOM's death. Grace takes some pills.

GRACE: (*Sarcastically.*) Just trying to have a religious experience.

TONY: Please don't take too many.

GRACE: (*Snaps out of all proportion.*) Don't tell me what to do Tony!

Beat. Recovers but not fully.

Are you going to leave me?

TONY: No.

GRACE: It's just I thought you might need to. Because of…

TONY: No.

GRACE: ...of how I've been behaving.

TONY: Yeah.

Beat.

GRACE: If I were you I'd...

TONY: You're not me.

GRACE: Perhaps you should think about it.

TONY: Don't tell me what to do Grace.

GRACE: No... (*You're right...*) Sorry.

They look at each other.

I couldn't let...

TONY: I know...

GRACE: Tom's funeral. I couldn't let...

TONY: I'm not sure we were right about that.

GRACE: Tony. I keep seeing him.

Beat.

TONY: Call Ruth.

GRACE: I can't.

TONY: Call Ruth and say sorry.

GRACE: I can't.

TONY: What was it the guy said?

GRACE: Who?

TONY: The Goldi Apparatus man.

GRACE: Golgi.

TONY: *Golgi.* What did he say? 'My dear fellow, I wish to thank you, I have been wrong these 25 years.' You clapped your hands red.

GRACE: (*This is why she loves him.*) How come you remember that?

TONY: Don't know. It's an inspiring story. Call Ruth.

GRACE looks at her husband.

Moves fluidly into:

Scene 14

TOM at seminary, giving a sermon.

TOM: But I think that we've got to stop thinking about God as a proper name, for a *thing*, as if the word God refers to some sort of object in the universe. And in fact, I think it's quite easy to demonstrate that God is not a *thing* at all. If you trawled the world y'know, if you made a manifest of all the things in the universe including tables and chairs and flowers and stones, there would not be on that list a thing called God. And actually I think that is there straightforwardly in the Bible...which is... I mean the great story of what God is like in the Bible, it seems to me, is the story of the Golden Calf and Moses going up the mountain. So you get the mountain, you get Moses going up the mountain – *this is the great story of religion I think* – Moses travels up the mountain. The higher he gets up the mountain, it gets cloudier and cloudier and cloudier, so the nearer to God, the nearer to this other, he gets less and less able to see, less and less able to know his way about, okay, down below, okay, what's happening down below is that all of them are making God into this thing, a Golden Calf and they're trying to make, y'know, it's like they're trying to make God into this physical thing. So you've got this contrast. The journey to the real divine which involves lostness, y'know, *doubt*, not being able to see, not being able to grasp this, this notion of God, this *no-thinglyness*. And yet, at the bottom of the mountain there's this sort of real thing and they all bow down to it. But it's a con. And the whole story is saying that God isn't like any *thing* we expect. And that's why it pisses me off when the atheists keep on trying to tell me what sort of God I believe in. It pisses me off that they assume what I believe. Because they want me to believe in a thing called God. But I don't. I don't believe God is a thing. I just believe in God.

Moves fluidly into:

Scene 15

Music begins. RUTH enters wearing an iPod, carrying a bag and drinking from an open bottle of cider. The music we can hear is what she is listening to: Ani DiFranco's 'Untouchable Face', from her live album Living in Clip. *RUTH sings along to the track. During this we spend a little time watching TONY who enters and is sitting in time for the second verse. He has woken up once again in the middle of the night. He wears a dressing gown and slippers and has come downstairs to think about his son. RUTH and TONY do not acknowledge one another. During the above autumn leaves fall followed by snow then blossom then green leaves then the red leaves of autumn again. And this journey through the seasons ends as GRACE enters to join RUTH at TOM's grave. Perhaps a small bench helps mark the place. RUTH doesn't notice GRACE at first then does. At a good moment RUTH sees GRACE and pulls the earphones from her ears. When she does so the music stops.*

RUTH: Sometimes I just need to use other people's words.

GRACE: Has Tony done this?

RUTH: Last year. He didn't sing, he said a prayer. In Hebrew. It was beautiful.

RUTH takes a plastic cup and an open packet of cigarettes from her shoulder bag. She fills the cup with cider from her bottle and passes it to GRACE.

Cider and cigarettes. To make you feel at home.

GRACE: Thank you.

RUTH: To… What was his name?

GRACE: Who?

RUTH: The initiator.

Beat.

GRACE: Kevin Johnston

RUTH: To Kevin Johnston.

GRACE: To Kevin.

Toast and drink.

Though to tell you the truth, he didn't actually initiate me. He tried his best but no cigar.

RUTH: I initiated Tom.

GRACE: Sorry?

RUTH: In a rowing boat.

GRACE: Gosh.

RUTH: Though initiation is a very generous way of putting it. I seem to remember it started off very well but… I only went out with him again out of pity. It was the beginning of my final term. I knew he liked me so I let him take me rowing.

GRACE: I feel embarrassed Ruth.

RUTH looks at her: 'Good'.

RUTH: Nowhere near as embarrassed as he did. He was a very proud boy, his mother's son after all.

GRACE: I'm sorry.

RUTH: (*Like a bullet.*) You really fucking should be. Two years Grace. You're a fucking idiot. With you and Tom it was always the same, it was always about love. Love, love, love. You loved your work. He loved his God. You loved your son. He loved his mother. God how he wanted your approval. He couldn't keep away, it was almost pathetic. And Tony. Poor Tony, he looks so sad now. Lost his sense of humour but – and how you love Tony is so weird – but I know how much he loves you. And that's why I loved Tom and his fucked up family because of all that passionate love whooshing around. And I did love it, love you all, even you who were so fucking rude all the time, I even loved you... But y'know, I'm less sure about love these days, less sure that it's the most important thing because it's just too much sometimes. Just too unmanageable – Don't you find? – Unmanageable to the point of – *I* do – because it so easily becomes and it does become, it really does, it becomes ferocious. I see it every day. I even see it in court. Cornered animals. Wounded and wilful and what for, I think love mostly. Love. And what is it? I mean *you* could tell me Grace, couldn't you, of course you could, you could describe it, use the correct language, delineate and separate and *explain*, explain this thing, this feeling. This feeling that we can't do anything much about except inflict on other people. Or try not to but that's very difficult. That's the problem. And I do understand, I get it. I do, I get it. I look at little Chan and she's so helpless and she's mine and my responsibility and I get it over and over and over. Overwhelmed. Overwhelmed. And I choke on it. Every day. And that's why I think it's wrong, completely wrong to give love such status, such *celebrity* when it's just so unbelievably dangerous, I would kill for that child. Kill. Not a problem. No hesitation. For her I would destroy. Absolutely. Mutilate someone. Like Tom was mutilated. You know. And I think. I'm coming to think, *believe* in fact, that it's kindness Grace – kindness, that's the big one, not love. That's what I'm coming to believe Grace, and it's

probably the more boring – definitely – kindness – because
it's calm and considerate and hesitant and certainly the
more difficult one to do. I find anyway. I really do. And
I might not have had much love at home but I had that
and I didn't even notice. It didn't even occur until... My
Mum. Remember, you said Tom told you. Do you? Well I
didn't understand... (*To the sky.*) And I'm sorry Mum that
I didn't but I do now and I think you were actually trying
to be *kind* Mum and I'm... Before she killed herself she
typed out letters for me and Dad and she couldn't type so
it must have taken her a long time and a lot of planning
so she must have given her suicide a great deal of thought
and wanted to leave everything just so, in a certain way,
she re-did her will, cleared out her cupboards and get this,
she threw away her perfumes. Her perfumes. All of them.
Threw them away. You know, so we wouldn't have to smell
her. (*To the sky.*) And Mum I didn't understand but I think
you were actually trying to be kind... And I'm proud... I
am Mum, I'm proud of...

RUTH stops.

But I'm not you see. Am I Grace? I'm just not... Fucking
hell. Every year I try. Every year and now with... Fifteen
years Mum. Fifteen fucking years! And I can't say it Mum
because I don't mean it! Because I'm not *proud* of you!
Not at all! I don't even want to understand you. Because
I'm still untrusting and closed and angry, always angry
because of you, because you were a *coward* Mum and you
didn't want to understand me. And you killed Dad and you
fucked me Mum, you totally *fucked* me and look at what's
happened. I go off in search of extremes like a magnet.
Ha! And I found them. I did. I found them. I found them
in college, I found them at work and most of all I found
them with her son. And I don't want to smell you anymore
Mum, I want to smell him. *Him!* And he's not here.
And you wanted to leave everything neat and tidy and I
didn't understand until they blew my life up...and what
happened to all those people. And Tom. Just because he

was there. Just because he was there. Just because he was there. What am I going to do? What the fuck am I... And when I started to love him and let him love me I thought I'd found what I'd been missing... and I lost him but this time with such a mess. Such a ferocious mess... And I thought about you Mum and how tidy you had been. And how still... Still.

I was baptised after she died. Never told Tom. Didn't last. And the thing is...that I think about is Tom... And I've waited until now to say it...waited for my chief witness to arrive because she was right about one thing Tom, she was right about me being a coward. Because...because I'm not sure I was going to be able to marry you. Really. I'm not sure I was going to be able to – He did ask me, of course he asked and I lied to you – because, because you didn't deserve the truth – because...because I suspect, and this *is* the truth Tom, I suspect you were going to love your God more than you were going to love me and... (*Shakes her head.*) And I've been thinking about that tortured man twisted on his cross and I understand the inspiration but, you know, I need to be the most important thing. I need that. Because of everything and... But we have a beautiful baby. We absolutely do. And she has your eyes and I'm okay when I look at them, most of the time...and I miss you...and I tell her about you or I try to, and your Dad does his dance move when he's singing her to sleep, and the Queen of Hearts is still down here swinging away with her axe and she has never seen her Granddaughter because...because...

RUTH sits down and takes a drink from the bottle. Eventually.

GRACE: I see him everywhere.

RUTH: Do you?

GRACE: Yes.

RUTH: I don't. Just in Chan.

Beat.

GRACE: (*Thinks she is helping RUTH.*) When Tom was born I understood something about life. That I wasn't at the centre of it anymore. It was a shock. Well, you know. You know exactly the strength of that feeling. And of course you could kill for that feeling. Tony always said so. And with having Tom...

RUTH: You should tell him.

GRACE: What?

RUTH: You should tell him.

GRACE: Talk to ghosts? Not really my style.

RUTH: (*Hard.*) Yeah? So how's your style been working for you Grace? Good is it?

Beat.

GRACE: And with having Tom...

RUTH: You.

GRACE: What?

RUTH: You. Having you...

GRACE: Don't bully me Ruth. I'm here.

RUTH: Try. And with having you...

GRACE: ...life seemed to make more sense.

RUTH: And with having you...

GRACE: Please...

RUTH: And with having you...

GRACE: (*Dominating and justifying.*) Life seemed to make more sense somehow. And I never told him. But I thought it was important, because you can't be there all the time and we have to learn, we have to know, that we're on our own in this world – there's no cosmic purpose – no plan...

RUTH: Enough Grace! Enough! And to think, you used to lecture me on being upfront.

RUTH makes to leave. She is stopped by GRACE's sudden anger.

GRACE: And all this faith! These promises of heavens and hells to come. *God!* Well it's absurd. It's absurd and dangerous and it's *wrong.* An overly simplistic, logic-chopping approach, Tom called it. He couldn't feel satisfied with the rational outlook. Wanted to turn violent religion into better religion. *Better* religion! (*GRACE looks at the sky and smiles.*) And somewhere inside me, so help me, some *splinter,* some *disgusting splinter* inside of me thinks, and so help me this is true, thinks that you Tom, you stupid, stupid, fucking…earnest, beautiful, beautiful boy of mine, that in some way you got what you deserved! (*Cracks beginning.*) Killed for a god! Murdered for a god! *You got what you deserved!* I'm sorry but I keep thinking it, I know it's not true but it's why I'm being so *cruel* to everyone who shows me anything but pain because I don't want pity, I want *scorn… I WANT SCORN…*

For the play to work it is essential that now GRACE's suppressed emotions crack through her and into the world. RUTH watches her for some time. Then she goes and sits beside her. Just sits. A picture of simple companionship. Time passes before…

RUTH: Who are you screaming at you mad woman?

GRACE: (*Laughs.*)

RUTH: Have you gone crazy, this is a churchyard.

GRACE: I'm sorry…

RUTH: Yeah right. Blow your nose, you're as bad as your granddaughter.

RUTH gives GRACE a hanky. GRACE blows her nose.

GRACE: A serious place for serious people.

RUTH: I dunno. I'm more with the gardener. Piss on the daisies.

GRACE: Geraniums.

RUTH: Geraniums. That was it. I'm going to light a candle.

GRACE nods.

You want to come? Even atheists need to light the occasional candle.

GRACE shakes her head.

GRACE: I'm just going to sit here for a while.

RUTH: Sure?

GRACE: Yeah.

RUTH: Okay. See you in a bit.

RUTH goes.

Beat.

Moves fluidly into:

Scene 16

TOM enters and sits beside his Mum. GRACE doesn't look at him. Some time passes before...

GRACE: I've been invited to Canada.

TOM: Canada?

GRACE: There's a neurologist out there trying to give people religious experiences.

TOM: In Canada?

GRACE: Mmm.

TOM: That sounds a bit suspicious if you ask me.

GRACE: You're as bad as your father. But Tony says I should go. Thinks it would do me good. Makes it sound like a Pilgrimage.

TOM: Could be.

Beat. For the first time in this exchange GRACE looks at her son. A moment. TOM smiles. GRACE fights back tears and smoothes TOM's hair with her hand.

How is he?

GRACE: He's sad son. He's really sad. He misses you terribly. He tries to hide it for my sake.

TOM: Poor Dad.

GRACE: And I've been no help. Working. Lecturing. Horrible. You can imagine.

TOM: Yeah.

GRACE: What do you mean *yeah?*

TOM: I mean yeah, I can imagine.

GRACE: Mmm.

TOM: How do they give it to you? The religious experience.

GRACE: (*Smiles.*) You have to wear this sort of motorcycle helmet...

TOM: Motorcycle helmet?

GRACE: Mmm, it holds the electrodes in the correct position.

TOM: Electrodes?

GRACE: Then they put these big black goggles over your eyes and get you to stare at a red light.

TOM: Big black goggles?

TOM exits. GRACE does not seem to notice.

GRACE: They're to reduce extraneous stimulation. Help the subject to concentrate apparently.

Beat where she alone hears TOM's reply. GRACE smiles.

They call it the God Helmet.

Crackle of Michael Persinger's speaker. Lights close in on GRACE.

Moves fluidly into:

MICHAEL: But you didn't see anything?

GRACE: Not exactly. It's more like feeling something, a *presence.*

MICHAEL: Like a ghost?

GRACE touches an ear with her hand.

Professor?

GRACE: It's difficult to explain.

MICHAEL: Well the process stimulated the right hemisphere of your brain in the region that controls ideas of self followed by the left hemisphere, the language centre, which usually interprets the stimulation as a sort of sensed entity.

GRACE smiles at the inadequacy of the explanation and nods her head –

GRACE: Right. Well that must have been it.

TONY and RUTH enter. RUTH brings on a small baby monitor and we move fluidly into:

Scene 17

The present. GRACE's home. The same location as Scene 2.

TONY: And this man actually gets paid to do this?

GRACE: He thinks it's this stimulation that's responsible for almost anything we sense as paranormal.

RUTH: *I see dead people.* What's that from? That one with thingy in it.

TONY: Don't know.

RUTH: Oh come on you do, that's going to drive me mad now.

TONY: Well I for one prefer life to have a little more mystery. And I refuse to let anyone reduce my sense of the spiritual to brain static.

GRACE: Especially a Canadian.

TONY: I thought you said it's just where he works?

GRACE: Come off it Tony. No one just works in Canada.

TONY: I knew it. The God Helmet! Talk about leading the witness.

RUTH: So who did you see?

Silence as the stage rests. Although TOM is no longer on stage his presence is felt by them all.

TONY: *(A gentle correction.)* Sense.

RUTH: Sorry. Sense. *The Sixth Sense!*

TONY: What?

RUTH: The name of the… *(TONY is not TOM.)* Nothing. Sorry. Who did you sense Grace?

TONY: Did you…*sense* anyone?

Beat.

GRACE: Well I… *(She looks from TONY to RUTH then back to TONY. She gathers herself. A fresh resolve, mostly for TONY's sake.)* No, it didn't really work on me. I just sort of felt floaty and remembered something Ruth had told me about her and Tom in a rowing boat.

TONY: A rowing boat?

RUTH: Grace!

GRACE: Yes?

TONY: What's this?

RUTH: Nothing. I can't believe you…

TONY: A Rowing Boat? Doesn't sound like nothing to me.

A speaker crackles. Though it is no longer Michael Persinger's speaker, but rather, the baby monitor through which CHAN can be heard crying.

RUTH: Oh here we go again.

TONY: Saved by the baby!

GRACE: I'll go.

TONY: No, stay where you are and talk behind my back. A rowing boat.

GRACE: No I mean I'd like to.

TONY stops.

(*To RUTH.*) If that's okay?

Beat.

RUTH: Yes. Grace. Yes of course it is.

Beat.

GRACE: Really?

RUTH nods her head. GRACE and RUTH share a moment. GRACE smiles and exits. TONY looks at RUTH and forces a smile. Then he looks to where GRACE has exited. He obviously has something on his mind.

RUTH: Are you okay?

TONY: Sometimes. You?

RUTH: Sometimes.

TONY: Thanks for coming.

RUTH: It's nice to see Grace.

TONY: Yeah. Em... Look... I found something the other day and I didn't know if I should just throw it away but in the end I didn't and em, well, here. (*TONY takes something from his pocket and hands it to RUTH. It is a napkin with a line down the middle and some writing on it.*)

RUTH: What is it? (*RUTH reads the napkin and realises what it is.*) 'She's cute.'

Beat.

Oh Tony...

A moment. Then through the speaker we hear:

GRACE: Hello there, and what's wrong with you? Yes. Yes. What's wrong with you? Come here and give Grandma a big hug, that's right, and then she'll tell you all about the *Blind Watchmaker.* Yes, you like the sound of that don't you. Blind Watchmaker!

TONY and RUTH look at each other: GRACE is unbelievable, relentless. Beat. Then we hear GRACE through the baby monitor. A clear change of tone, speaking now to her eavesdroppers.

GRACE: Bloody got you both didn't I! Blind Watchmaker! I got you! Ha! I know I got you. (*To CHAN.*) I know I got them...

TONY: (*Getting up. Lying.*) She didn't get me.

RUTH: (*Also lying.*) Me neither.

TONY: I'm starving. Do you want something to eat?

RUTH: Yeah. I'll come with you.

TONY: Come on.

TONY and RUTH exit.

GRACE: I got you! Yes, Grandma got them didn't she, yes she did, Grandma got them 'cause Grandma's very *clever* isn't she, yes… And just look at your beautiful, beautiful eyes, just look… (*Suddenly struck.*) Gosh. Exactly like your Dad. That's right love. Exactly like your Dad…

Several beats.

Lights down slowly.

End of play.